The Little Book of Sa:

If you are in need of a pick me up, consider **The Little Book of Sass** the sassy friend that everyone needs in life.

Hold a thought in your mind and select a page. Whether you are heartbroken, in need of some motivation or just want some positive vibes to start your day, the page you select is bound to cheer you up.

Stay sassy xxx

Sassy Book Club

I know you are super keen for that motivation but before you read my book why not join my sassy book club?

It is completely free to join and it will give you the chance to get free copies of my future books.

To join, just email me: info@meerasharma.com
(You can even just send a blank email)

There's no spam: I only send out a 2 to 3 emails a year and I will never sell your details.

Anyway, without further ado, enjoy my book and get ready for some sassy motivation. #sasspirational

You have a few hours in the day were you are allowed to be emotional. After that suck it up and be a sassy boss. That means now…yep, go and channel that inner sassy boss.

Girl, you do not need that person in your life. There are so many better people out there who will appreciate you for being you. You are a sassy individual who is complete within. Remember, you do not need anyone's validation.

You are a strong, sassy woman of substance.
It's difficult to break a real, sassy woman because you learn from your mistakes and you turn those mistakes into strengths. So go do that. Bam.

Sassy women rarely do tears, but when they do they cry tears of glitter. Yeah, you are so fantastic, even when you cry.

What are you worrying and stressing about? Last time I checked you are a sassy woman and don't stress about things as it doesn't change the situation. Sassy women rarely let things overwhelm them, but if they do they take a moment to breathe in, breathe out and find a solution like a boss. There is always a solution to your problem. Remember that.

You can achieve whatever you set your mind to achieve. It's all about your mindset so change your mindset. Don't think you can't do it - think you can. Nothing is impossible. Remember you are sassy so you can achieve everything you can possibly imagine. Go get those dreams, girlfriend.

You can't change things that happen to you, you can only change how you react to a situation. Rather than getting stressed or angry about it chill, think positive and positive things will happen.

Remember it could be a blessing in a disguise. Things happen for a reason. You will look back on this day and realize it happened for the best so pick yourself up and put that sassy smile back on.

Remember sass, everything is about our thinking: look at everything that is currently holding you back as temporary. If you think it is not permanent, it won't be. If you think you can reach so much more than you imagined then you can! Think you can do boot camp on a Sunday morning and you will....you can do EVERYTHING. You are sass!

Go do those squats so your ass matches your sass.

Go work out, look hot and then be sassy. Remember you won't get the butt you want by sitting on it! You will never regret working out.

Missing someone? Call them. Want to meet up with someone? Ask them. Love someone? Tell them. Feeling sassy? Be sassy. It's as easy as that. No more complications.

What are you worrying about? Rather than thinking about how it can go wrong, focus on how it will go right. Stay positive and sassy.

When you are being you, don't waste a moment thinking about what others will think. Instead, reflect on what is driving you to waste your time on worrying about what others will think. If you are not harming anyone with your actions then who cares! Stay sassy, be you and do you!

Shake it off. Throw some glitter on it and stay happy and sassy.

Feeling down about something? Breathe in, breathe out and then visualize glitter on the situation. Better already, right?

Tell those negative thoughts in your mind to shut the hell up. Then go put your sassy top on and take on the world!

You are sassy so you never dwell on the past. Shit happens, learn from it and move on.

The only time you should ever look back on life is to see how far you have come, and sass, you have come far!

Spread the sassy love today. Be that person that brightens up someone else's day!

Keep shining, smiling and stay sassy.

No one can make you feel bad or inferior without your consent. Why are you letting someone upset you? Remember sass, their comments and opinions are their opinions, NOT yours! Throw some glitter and shake it off.

Sassy women don't need validation from others. So set those goals, stay quiet, smash those goals out of the park and then give yourself a sassy clap.

Never run for a train, a bus or a man because when one leaves another arrives. Remember sass, things happen for the best. You may not see it now but a few days, weeks or months down the line you will.

Get up, work out, dress up, add some sass and don't let anyone make your crown slip. Today is your day, you sassy queen.

This is a reminder that you are intelligent, funny, motivated, beautiful, and sassy. So go be that.

Those who leave a trail of sassy glitter are never forgotten ;)

In case you forgot, sassy = someone endowed with an ungodly amount of cool. Yep, that is you.

You are fun, daring, sexy, someone everyone wants to know, yep you are sassy.

This is your daily reminder that you are someone who is cheeky, lively, smart, energetic, chatty and a bit bad-assy. You are the definition of sass.

No matter what you believe
you only live once, so you
might as well just do
whatever makes you happy.
So just go do it and be sassy.

Don't let anyone steal your happiness or tell you not to be sassy.

Sass, being happy is an inside job. Don't give anyone power over your feelings or life. Smile.

Have faith. Keep trying. Laugh at your problems. Drink your smoothie. Work out. Stay happy and stay sassy.

Want to do something, sass?
Then go do it. Simple as.

Blablablabla. There sass, excuses are over – now go work out.

Remember sass, you are what you eat so please don't be cheap, easy, fast or fake.

Life is like the weather. Just because it rains now and then it doesn't mean the sun never comes out. Behind those dull days is something sunny, spectacular, and of course sassy ;)

How wonderful is it that some of the best days of your life haven't happened yet. You have so much to look forward to my sassy friend.

Complaining about things constantly doesn't help a situation. It stops positivity coming into your life. Moan about it for no more than a minute, find a solution, move on, and stay sassy.

Book yourself that flight,
explore the world and spread
sassiness, love, and light.

Don't forget why you started. Keep your head high, your crown straight and carry on.

Just because someone said you couldn't do it, doesn't mean you can't! Go do it and prove them wrong. You are sassy after all and you can do everything you put your mind to!

You are worth so much, so stop fretting and giving people so much influence over your life.

Erm, why are you comparing yourself to others? Remember you are unique, funny and sassy in your own way.

Stop concerning yourself with what others are doing. Sassy women do not care what others are doing.
Concentrate on your own life and make it great.

Sassy women do not concern themselves with other people's lives and negativity. You have a choice so choose to step back and not let someone's negativity spoil your energy.

Today sass, walk around like you are an 11/10 because girl you are!

Confidence has no competition – the only person you should be competing with is yourself. Make today better than yesterday.

Today is the day you turn those sassy dreams into a reality. Remember nothing is impossible.

Sassy women don't tip toe, they strut around like they mean it.

Intelligence and confidence are two of the most beautiful attributes a person can have. Oh yeah, and being sassy....;) Don't forget you have all those traits.

No drama, no negativity, just be positive today and every day. Simple. As.

If you are doubting yourself, remember you can do it. Look at your life and see how far you have come. Most importantly remember that you are sassy and the world is your oyster.

Being nice is free so go sprinkle niceness everywhere…and some glitter, throw some glitter around.

Your vibe attracts your tribe so keep your vibe positive and sassy. Word.

Sass, you are the reason someone smiles. Nice right?

Sass, in case you need a reminder - your figure is perfect, your personality is fab, your smile lights up a room and you are intelligent! You are doing an amazing job at life so don't forget that.

Why are you thinking so much about it? If you want to do something do it. Nothing can hold you back.

Each day is a fresh start, a new beginning to work towards those dreams and live the life you want to live. Amazing, right?

Your story and sassiness is unique so why are you comparing yourself to others? Today is the day you stop comparing.

Don't let your success get to your head. Sassy women always stay humble.

Don't let failure get you down. Learn from it and work harder. You can do it sass!

Every accomplishment starts with the will to try so make today the day you work hard towards your goals. Keep it up, sass!

Sometimes you just need a bit of time to yourself. Make today the day where you pamper yourself and relax.

Remember sassy women don't get mad or get even. They just do much better and work so hard, which allows them to forget all the bad things that happened to them. Yep, they let their success do the talking.

Sass, stay focused on your goal. Don't let anyone say you can't achieve it because this is your reminder that you can!

Nothing can stop a determined and sassy woman so strut towards those dreams.

There are plenty of ways to achieve your dreams, just find the way. Remember if you run into a wall in life just figure a way to climb over that biatch.

Confidence is not about whether they like you, it's about being cool if they don't. Who cares what people think? Not you.

People are always going to stare and talk so you might as well make it worth their while sass. ;)

Don't doubt yourself. Remember it's not *who you are* that holds you back. It's *who you think you are not.* Believe in your sassy self.

You can spend hours, days, weeks and months over-analyzing situations. Well, this is your reminder to let it go and move on with your life.

You only live once so make it a good one. Just do it.

Sassy women believe it is better to look back on life and think "Hell, I can't believe I did that," than looking back and thinking "Dang, I wish I did that."

Some people want things to happen; others wish it would happen whilst sassy women make it happen.

About the Author

Meera Sharma is the founder of The School of Sass, which she launched to educate everyone on the skills they need to stay motivated, positive and thus live their sassiest lives.

Meera believes that everyone can live their best life. However she also acknowledges we can all have a down day, which is exactly when we need someone to cheer us on. This inspired her to publish The Little Book of Sass, featuring *sasspirational* quotes to perk people up when they need it the most.

For daily #sasspirational follow Meera on Instagram @theschoolofsass

Copyright

Printed in Poland
by Amazon Fulfillment
Poland Sp. z o.o., Wrocław

50478743R00047